Insects Change

by Lisa Trumbauer

Harcourt Achieve
Rigby • Steck-Vaughn

www.HarcourtAchieve.com
1.800.531.5015

All of these creatures are insects.
They are **adults**.

All of these creatures are insects, too.
They are **young** insects.
Insects change as they grow.

A **butterfly** changes as it grows.
First, a **caterpillar** hatches from an **egg**.
Then, the caterpillar changes into a **chrysalis**.
Finally, the chrysalis changes into a butterfly.

egg
caterpillar
chrysalis
butterfly

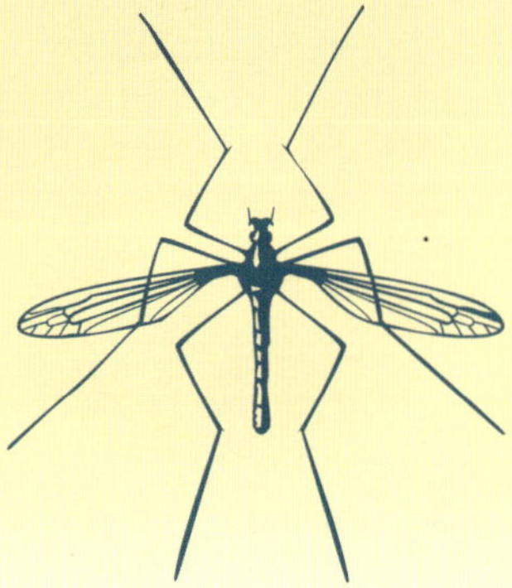

A **mosquito** changes as it grows.
First, a **wriggler** hatches from an **egg**.
Then, the wriggler changes into a **pupa**.
Finally, the pupa changes into a mosquito.

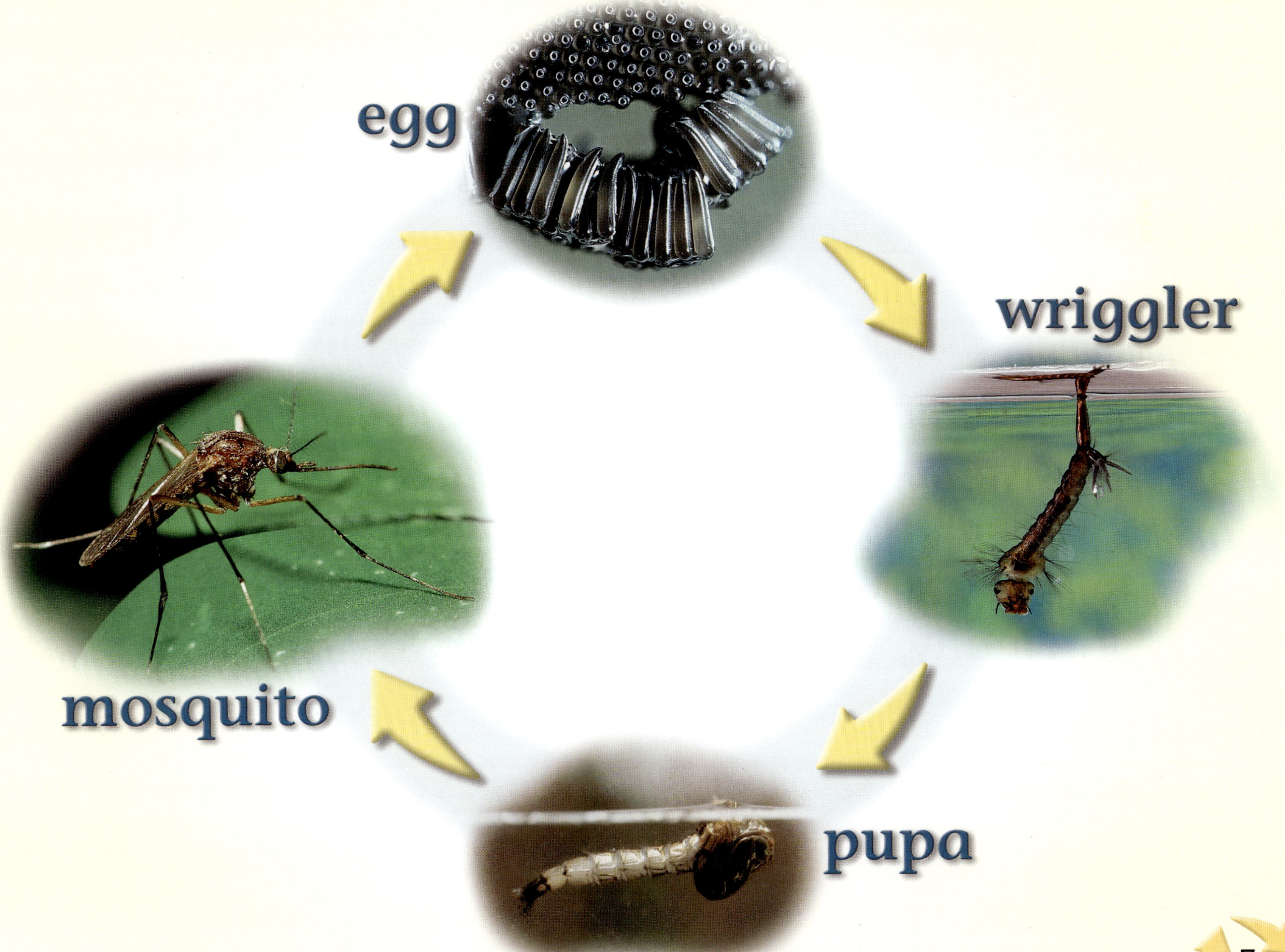
egg
wriggler
pupa
mosquito

An **ant** changes as it grows.
First, a **larva** hatches from an **egg**.
Then, the larva changes into a **pupa**.
Finally, the pupa changes into an ant.

egg
larva
pupa
ant

A **bee** changes as it grows.
First, a **larva** hatches from an **egg**.
Then, the larva changes into a **pupa**.
Finally, the pupa changes into a bee.

egg
larva
pupa
bee

A **dragonfly** changes as it grows.
First, a **nymph** hatches from an **egg**.
The nymph lives in or near water.
Finally, the nymph changes into a dragonfly.

egg
nymph
dragonfly

A **grasshopper** changes as it grows.
First, a **nymph** hatches from an **egg**.
As the nymph changes, wings grow.
Finally, the nymph changes into a grasshopper.

egg
nymph
grasshopper

One day, the female grasshopper will lay eggs.
Then a new family of grasshoppers will hatch.